The Single Moms
Little Book of Wisdom

Other Books By The Author

Cool, Confident and Strong: 52 Power Moves for Girls. ($12.95)

Give girls that tools they need to build healthy self-esteem and make smart dating and relationship choices. This book provides pre-teen and teenage girls with the tools they need to make decisions that respect their values and boundaries.

Young, Gifted and Doing It: 52 Power Moves for Teens. ($14.95)

Give your teenagers the tools they need to succeed with this success guide for teens. From resisting negative peer pressure to goal setting to developing a clear sense of purpose, this book provides teens with a basic blueprint that they can utilize to position themselves for life-long success and achievement.

Smart Moves That Successful Youth Workers Make. ($24.95)

This book will show you how to become a highly effective youth worker. You'll learn: the seven roles of the front-line youth worker and how to manage each, how to avoid the ten most common mistakes that youth workers make and how to build assets in youth that have a lasting impact.

Her Rite of Passage: How to Design & Deliver A Rites of Passage Program for African-American Girls and Young Women. ($39.95)

This book will show you how to set up a rites of passage program from start to finish. It includes a 42-session workshop curriculum based on the principles of Kwanzaa and offers step-by-step guide-lines for planning and carrying out an initiation retreat and crossover ceremony.

The Single Moms
Little Book of Wisdom

♦

42 Tidbits of Wisdom To Help You Survive, Succeed and Stay Strong

Cassandra Mack

iUniverse, Inc.
New York Lincoln Shanghai

The Single Moms Little Book of Wisdom
42 Tidbits of Wisdom To Help You Survive, Succeed and Stay Strong

iUniverse books may be ordered through booksellers or by contacting:

iUniverse
2021 Pine Lake Road, Suite 100
Lincoln, NE 68512
www.iuniverse.com
1-800-Authors (1-800-288-4677)

The views expressed in this work are solely those of the author and do not necessarily reflect the views of the publisher, and the publisher hereby disclaims any responsibility for them.

ISBN-13: 978-0-595-39752-5 (pbk)
ISBN-13: 978-0-595-84159-2 (ebk)
ISBN-10: 0-595-39752-2 (pbk)
ISBN-10: 0-595-84159-7 (ebk)

Printed in the United States of America

Contents

Acknowledgements

I feel so blessed and privileged to be able to fulfill my heart's desire and do what I love. I thank God for giving me the vision and inspiration to write this book. I thank my family who has always supported me, in one way or another. I thank my mother for giving me a firm foundation and standing by me when I needed it the most. I thank the father who raised me, Eddie Ramsey for teaching me by example what I should look for in a divine mate. I thank my aunts, Vera, Valerie, Idella and Norma for their wisdom, honest advice and insight. Chris Moore, you are my rock.

Alfonso Wyatt, thank you for calling me to come up higher and for advising me on so many important issues. Robyn Brown-Manning and Larry Mack, thank you for opening up doors for me. Shawn Dove, thank you for motivating the motivator and believing in my dreams enough to always back me. Deborah Cofer, thank you for just being you. Through your diligence and dedication you inspire me to keep on pursuing my goals. Gessy, thank you for always encouraging me and praying me through so many situations. Janet Aiken, thank you for always coming through during the midnight hour and speaking so many blessings over my life. Candice, thank you for bringing laughter into my life and listening to my crazy ideas. Kim Dennis, for opening the very first door for me. Scott Thompson, thank you for making sure that I always had work by continually inviting me to present workshops at HSW.

Thank you, KC for all of your wise KC'isms, your spiritual encouragement and support throughout the years, Deidre for helping me to let my hair down and take off the cape, Yvette for our long talks about life, love and happiness and for never saying I told you so even when you knew in advance, Marylou for your constant thoughtfulness and Mia for always keeping it real with me. To my sister, Kaydia and brother, Khasai success is in your hands. All you have to do is follow your heart. To my son Briston, you are the wind beneath my wings.

Encouragement for the Journey

Being a single mom comes with many challenges. You've got to make it happen for you and your children. You've got numerous demands on your time. Your resources are stretched to the limit. You've got to make sure that you are able to stay financially afloat even though money is often critically tight. And with all of this on your plate, it's also important that you still find time to laugh, love and pursue some of your own goals and dreams.

As a single mom myself, I share many of your challenges and understand the pressures you face. Between chasing after my two-year old son, finding time to write and develop material for my workshops and trying to have some semblance of a personal life, I have to be very disciplined around creating blocks of time to work on myself and pursue some of my own dreams. At first, I used to feel guilty about my "me time." I even wondered if I was neglecting my son in the process. But I have now come to realize that when I take time to do me, I become a more patient and balanced mother who can provide a more loving, nurturing and stable environment for my child.

The Single Moms Little Book of Wisdom, is an inspirational book of wise sayings that will help you to step into your greatness, maintain grace under pressure, hold on to motherhood with both hands, let go of excess baggage and prepare yourself for the best kind of love.

The Single Moms Little Book of Wisdom, was written for the busy, single mom who is short on time but long on dreams and looking for some encouragement for the journey. *The Single Moms Little Book of Wisdom,* offers 42 wise sayings that will motivate, inspire and encourage you so that you can succeed, survive and stay strong.

It is my hope that *The Single Moms Little Book of Wisdom*, gives you the wisdom, encouragement and extra push you need to go after your dreams with boldness, let go of the things you need to let go of and enjoy everyday life. You deserve it.

See you on the path,

Cassandra Mack

1

Stepping Into Your Greatness

Wise Saying #1.
Develop An Unshakeable Belief In Yourself and Your Ability To Live Your Dreams

Did you know that right where you are you have the power to create the life you want—to live your dreams, feel more fulfilled, put some of the stress to rest, accomplish your goals, provide for your children and design the kind of life that you can feel good about? You really do have power, because a quality life starts on the inside. It's not about how much money you have, where you live, how prestigious your career is or how much education you have. It's about your mindset—your beliefs, your willpower and your attitude. So, if you are going to succeed and stand strong as a single mother, two things need to happen: First, you must believe in your heart of hearts that you can make it as a single mother no matter what things look like externally. This is your faith walk. Second, you must know in the core of your soul that it is possible to achieve your goals and live your vision. This is divine grace coupled with purpose. When these two things come together: faith and divine grace coupled with purpose, you have the foundation to create a life worth living.

What's important for you to know is that there are thousands, if not hundreds of thousands of single mothers, some with more resources, others with less, who are blazing trails, excelling in their careers, starting businesses, going back to school, purchasing homes and achieving things they've never achieved before. Life doesn't play favorites. So if they are doing it, then you can do it too.

Believe it or not, success really is a mindset. It starts on the inside with your beliefs then extends to your outer world with your choices and habits. Whether you call it confidence, self-esteem or the power of positive thinking, it all comes down to believing that you have what it takes to not only make it, but to make it on your terms. It's also knowing that whatever you don't have you can borrow, barter for, outsource or learn.

If you believe in your abilities, nurture your dreams and act as if it is possible to live the life you envision, then you will do what is necessary to bring about your desired results. The opposite is also true. If you believe that you do not have what it takes to be successful, then your own self-limiting beliefs will prevent you from going after your dreams.

You have too much to offer and too much to do for yourself and your children to allow limited thinking to sabotage your success. Today, remind yourself that you've got strengths, talents and abilities that are valuable and marketable. You have what it takes to make it.

Wise Saying #2.
Become The Author of Your Story

What's the secret to getting from where you are now to where you want to be? It's becoming the author of your story. Taking 100% responsibility for the direction and quality of your life. If you want your life to go in a different direction, then it's up to you to take yourself there. That means starting where you are, working with what you've got and choosing action over feelings.

It's important to develop the mindset that you have the power to take a different route, try a new thing, make your life better, get it right this time and step away from people and situations that bring you down and hinder your growth. Becoming the author of your story is about acknowledging that you do have power because you were created by the Ultimate Power Source. Becoming the author of your story means that you decide whether your life will unfold like a horror story, an urban tale, a suspense novel, a comedy, tragedy or an action-adventure.

As the author of your story, you decide which chapters to write, which ones to omit and which ones to completely close out. You decide who the main characters are and what role they will play. And the most empowering part of it all is, if you do not like the way your story is playing out, you can always make a few revisions, come out with a new edition or write an entirely different book. Today, become the author of your story and see how wonderfully your life unfolds.

Wise Saying #3.
Resist The Urge To Pick Yourself Apart

Where did we ever get the idea that we had to be perfect? That we had to have it all figured out by a certain age and time. A huge, sometimes overwhelming source of stress for women is the need for everything and everyone to be perfect. When we buy into this irrational kind of thinking, we place unrealistic demands on ourselves and set ourselves up for disappointment. How? Because, if we are busy picking ourselves apart and focusing on who we are not and what we do not have, then we will never be content or be able to see the good in our lives. As a result, we become dissatisfied with life.

Nobody has it all figured out all the time. Not even the people who think they do. Everyone has moments of doubt and insecurity. This is a normal part of the human experience. The problem comes in when doubt and insecurity become the norm and lead us to set impossible standards or deadlines that are not realistic with our time and energy constraints or the resources we have at hand.

Instead of striving for perfection, why not strive for excellence and balance. Today, give yourself credit for all that you do. Take inventory of your blessings. Give yourself a pat on the back for just being you.

Wise Saying #4.
Dream Big Dreams and Pursue Them Passionately

Far too many women spend countless days, weeks and hours daydreaming about the lives they wish they had. We spend our waking hours daydreaming and our sleeping hours worrying about what tomorrow might bring. We look back with regret wondering about what could have been, what should have been or beating ourselves up for all the things we failed to do. Nothing kills your spirit quicker than looking at life through the lens of regret. The best way to avoid living a life of would haves, could haves and should haves is to dream big dreams and commit yourself to the pursuit of your dreams. All it takes is one step to get started. Once you take the first step, you are halfway there.

Just for today, imagine that there were no limits to hold you back. What would you do? Would you start that business you've always dreamed about? Plan a trip to Europe, Africa or the Caribbean? Would you go back to school? Get a patent for that invention you've been toying with? Learn another language? Write your memoirs? Well, the time to do it is now. Not when you lose twenty-five pounds, find a husband or when the kids are off on their own. Pursuing your dreams is not a selfish thing. It's a self-care thing. Plus, when you pursue your dreams no matter where you are in life, you show your children that it's never too late to follow your heart.

Believe it or not, your imagination is a powerhouse of possibility. It can be used to create the kind of life that others only dream of. Dream big dreams. Hold a picture in your mind's eye of you achieving your dreams. Let this be the catalyst for pursuing your passions or at least some of the items on your wish list. Keep thinking about your dreams. Keep talking about your dreams. Then take the necessary steps to move your dream from a fantasy inside your head into a tangible reality.

If there's a goal you've been wanting to accomplish or a dream that's locked deep in your heart today is your day to go for it. Who knows? You just might succeed.

Wise Saying #5.
Start Where You Are

Whenever I think about the principle of starting where you are, I think of the biblical story in the book of Exodus where God calls on Moses and informs him that he will be leading the Israelites out of Egypt. This was a big and scary task. Pharaoh was a powerful enemy. And Moses felt like he was not equipped to handle the challenge. He pleaded with God to let him off the hook. But God did not allow Moses' fear or apprehension to prevent him from fulfilling his mission. God simply asked Moses, "What do you have in your hand?" Moses replied, "A shepherd's staff." God used the shepherd's staff to give Moses the confidence and courage he needed to answer the call.

The powerful lesson that I take from this story is the only way to get started on your success is to start where you are. What ordinary things do you have on hand right now to help get you started—a library to start the research, a pen and notebook to write your ideas down, a computer, a good friend you can bounce ideas off of, a voice to start talking to people about your plans and dreams, a car or bus fare to get out of the neighborhood for a while so that you can think clearly, your children to motivate you to aim higher? As you can see, you already got the basics to get started.

It's easy to assume that you cannot begin working towards your dreams until every "i" is dotted, every "t" is crossed and all your ducks are lined up in a row. But the truth is you can start right now if you choose to start where you are. As long as you've got a sound mind and a burning desire to live your dreams then you've got the prerequisites to get you started. Today, make the decision to start where you are.

Wise Saying #6.
Let Others Keep Their Criticism,
You Keep Your Dreams

As you walk the path of success, you will meet many different kinds of people. Some people will encourage you, celebrate your achievements and give you constructive feedback that you can use for your betterment. Others will check on you from time to time to see how you're doing and make sure that you and the kids are ok. Still others are too preoccupied with their own lives to concern themselves with your success. Then there are those who fancy themselves as critics. They almost always have something negative to say about you, your dreams and your choices. These are the very people you have to watch out for, because if you are not careful their poisonous comments can pollute your spirit and cause you to second-guess yourself.

This is why it is so important that you guard your dreams from dream killers. Do your best to consistently and continually surround yourself with positive people who are real, the kind of people who lift you up and support you. It's important to keep in mind that the thoughts we hold in our heads are like seeds. And if we allow weeds to mix and mingle with our seeds, they can destroy all that we have planted and cultivated. Sometimes, before our garden ever has a chance to come into full bloom.

Everyone has to learn to manage negativity in his or her own way. What I have found to be helpful for me is to turn my haters into my motivators. Sounds crazy, I know. But even negative feedback can be helpful if you keep it in its proper perspective, remember the source it comes from, and use it to step up your game. The important thing to keep in mind is that people can have their opinions of you, but you have the final word on your dreams.

Wise Saying #7.
Success is 10% Imagination and 90% Perspiration

Jane has a knack for doing hair. She's quite good at it. Jane has big dreams, great ideas and hopes to one day open up her own beauty salon. Every now and then, she takes a workshop or reads an insider's magazine, but for the most part she does little to move herself closer to her dream of becoming a beauty shop owner. Jane is a single mother of two teenage boys. She's in an on again, off again relationship that leaves her drained and unfulfilled. Currently, Jane works as a receptionist at a marketing firm, but her passion is styling hair.

Many people despite good intentions and extraordinary talent fail to achieve the things they long to achieve because of their unwillingness to put in the work. Every action you take towards your goals counts. Every task you perform that is related to your goals is like making a deposit in your success account. Usually when we meet people who've done well for themselves we think of them as being smarter or more talented than we are. But the reality is the results that they have achieved are the consequences of discipline, effective time management and a detailed action-plan.

Many of us squander the little time we have on trivial things and trivial people who are not consistent with where we want to be or who do not positively contribute to our lives. There's no getting around it. Success is about choices. When you convert your wishes into plans and your good intentions into goals, you'll almost always achieve your desired results. Here are some steps to help you build your sweat equity.

Step 1. Decide What You Want
What do you want out of life? What kinds of experiences do you want to have? How do you want to feel? What do you want to achieve? What do you want for and from your family?

Step 2. Develop A Clear Sense of Purpose

What do you believe you were put on this earth to do? What do you feel clearly certain of? What do you feel called or compelled to do? What's the reason behind everything you do? When do you feel most joyful, fulfilled and in sync with your spirit?

Step 3. Create A Goals Book

What do you want to accomplish and by when? Be as specific and clear here as possible. It's not enough to have one goal. In order to maximize your quality of life, you need to have goals for every area of your life—personal, financial, career, family and social life. Set goals that will stretch you and help you to grow personally as well as professionally. Break your goals down into bite-sized, action steps.

Step 4. Learn As Much As You Can

Did you know that the average American watches about six hours of television per day? If this is you, that time could be better spent learning and growing. The more you learn the more tools you have at your disposal, the more marketable you become in the workplace and the more you elevate your game.

Step 5.Get Ready

What do you need to do to get ready—to position yourself for success? Do you need to develop a new skill? Go back to school? Take a class or workshop? Get your money right? Develop healthier habits? Whatever you need to do to get ready, start now by writing down three to five things that you will commit to doing this week in order to position yourself for success.

2

Grace Under Pressure

Wise Saying #8.
You're Not The First and You're Not The Last

You're going through a messy divorce. In fact, messy is an understatement for the recent hell you've been through. You're dividing up assets. Fighting over the children. Reviewing financial statements. Communicating with one another through attorneys. And the mistress whom your husband told the marriage counselor he was no longer seeing is dutifully standing by his side. Her make-up applied to perfection. Hair coiffed without a strand out of place, waiting like a vulture to get her hands on what took you twenty years to build.

Perhaps you're the president of the Usher Board. You never imagined that you would have a child outside of marriage. But the baby is on its way. Your belly is growing. The congregation is starting to whisper. And it doesn't help matters that the father of your soon-to-be bundle of joy is married to somebody else.

No matter what situation you find yourself in. No matter how many times you've told yourself that this would never happen to you. No matter how bad you feel, how stupid you look, how scared you are or how disappointed others are in your actions, you are not the first to go through your situation and you are certainly not the last. So before you do anything foolish or rash, call on God and seek the wisdom you need to move forward. God will continue to love you. God will give you the strength you need to get through whatever it is that you are going through. And God will forgive you, even when everyone else is ready to throw you to the wolves. Today, know that you are not alone.

Wise Saying #9.
You Can't Save Your Face And Your Ass
At The Same Time

One of the hardest things that Pat had to do was sit in a pre-screening social service center with tax returns and pay stubs in hand to see if she and her three children qualified for food stamps. Pat was smart. Had a college degree in psychology. As a former caseworker she often counseled women like this, but never thought in a million years that she would be walking in their shoes.

Being the proud diva that she was, Pat continually looked over her shoulder to make sure that no one she knew spotted her. And if they did, she had a halfway believable-sounding lie ready for them. Pat told herself that she was going through a temporary cash flow problem when the truth was she was dead broke. For Pat, appearances were everything. She fought hard to keep up the façade. But fronting has its price.

Cindy, on the other hand, is a successful lawyer with a stellar track record. She rarely lost a case. Her ex-boyfriend, Joe is dangerously obsessed with her, so much so that he leaves at least twenty messages a day and follows her to and from the office, even though it's been over between them for more than a year and she's made it absolutely clear that his behavior is making her uncomfortable. Cindy hasn't told anyone at the law firm about her "little situation" because she does not want her problem to interfere with the job. It doesn't help matters that she may have to seek protection from the very same courthouse that she litigates in.

There's an old saying that goes: *You can't save your face and your ass at the same time*. And without a doubt this saying is true. When you're in need of help, you are in need of help, no matter who you are, how much you know, how prestigious your reputation or how pulled together you appear to be. Something's got to give. And if you are not careful, that something could be you.

If you find yourself in a situation where your health, economic survival or safety is at risk, you cannot keep it hidden forever. Eventually, someone is going to notice. People really do pay attention. Somebody, somewhere is going to notice that something is wrong, that you are not your usual self, your work is slacking, your thoughts are drifting, you're more secretive, withdrawn, your habits have changed and that something is out of balance.

Just for a moment, step out of the keeping-up-appearances mode and go into save-you-ass mode. Forget about your prestige, image and social standing. They cannot help you. Collect your bearings. Get past the "what will people think" mindset. Pick up the phone and let someone know what's going on. And if at first you don't get the help you need, call someone else. If you let people know what's going on, I guarantee you someone in your network will know someone, who will know someone, that can help you. And someone else will know someone who has been right where you are now.

Wise Saying #10.
Your Child Is Not A Mistake
and You Are Not Destined for Welfare

Often when a woman has a child out of wedlock she is thought of as immoral, loose or less deserving than a woman whose children came by way of marriage. And if she is receiving any form of public assistance, even if it is used as a stepping stone to create a better life for her family she is often looked down upon. Ironically, the wealthy receive public assistance in the form of tax breaks. And whose tax dollars do you think pays for their welfare? Yet, you don't see too many people calling them lazy or immoral.

If you have a child outside of marriage, you need to know that your child is not a mistake or a burden to society. She might have been an unanticipated surprise, but she's no accident. No human being has the right to judge you, because none of us are without fault and none of us have a Heaven or Hell to cast you in. From this moment on focus on growing as a person, being a good mother and creating a quality life for yourself and your child.

With God's guidance and your determination you can groom your child for greatness. Today, know that your child is a blessing and you have what it takes to be a great mom.

Wise Saying #11.
When You Don't Know What Else To Do Pray

Prayer is the most powerful tool that you will ever have at your disposal. So when you feel like you are at your wits end and you don't know what else to do, pray. When life feels bad and your situation seems to be spinning out of control the smartest thing that you can do is pray. Prayer really does change things. If it doesn't change the situation, it will change your outlook and give you the strength to get through it.

The wonderful thing about prayer is that there is no single set way to pray. You can pray kneeling, standing, sitting down or lying down. You can pray any time of the day. You don't even have to think of a bunch of fancy words to say, just tell God what you're feeling and going through. If you don't know where to start, start by thanking God for allowing you to see another day. Because no matter how tough things are, every day above ground is certainly better than any day below it. Ask for God's grace and mercy. Ask God to fill your heart and mind with peace and goodness. Pray for guidance, wisdom, strength and courage. Pray for your children. Pray for people who are worse off than you. Even pray for people you don't like. They probably need it the most.

You may not see any tangible benefits right away. You may not even understand why you are going through whatever it is that you are going through, but if you keep the faith and turn your troubles over to God, things will eventually work out for your greater good.

Wise Saying #12.
You Don't Have To Do It All Alone

Where did we get the idea that we have to do it all alone? That we should never reach out for help, ask for support or admit that some burdens are too heavy to bear alone. It seems that super women have the toughest time letting others know that they cannot do it by themselves all the time. They have an even tougher time admitting that they are scared and at their wits end.

Speaking for myself as a recovering super woman, for the longest time I resisted letting others know how I was really feeling and doing. I smiled when I was feeling down I laughed when I wanted to cry. And I pretended that all was well in my world when everything around me was coming apart at the seams.

One of the most remarkable characteristics of the single mother is her ability to be resourceful. We're able to make a pot of rice and beans with neck bones taste like a five-course meal. We can jazz up a $39.99 outfit from Target and make it look like a runway hit. We can make birthdays and holidays memorable and special, even if we cannot afford to throw a big shindig or put presents underneath the tree. Resourcefulness is a wonderful asset, but never confuse the inability to ask for help with resourcefulness. They are not one and the same.

Today, take a load off. Let your hair down. Lighten up. Tell a friend how you're really feeling and doing. Ask for the resources you need. It's ok to play the super woman role sometimes. But today, give yourself permission to put down your lasso.

Wise Saying #13.
When All Hell Breaks Loose, Take Things One Step At A Time

What do you do when everything around you is coming apart at the seams—when the rent is past due, the creditors are calling and the eviction notice is just a few days away? What do you do when your children are in trouble again, you've got drama on the job, a negative report from the doctor and the man who you thought was Mr. Right turns out to be a wolf in sheep's clothing? You do what you can do, by taking things one step at a time.

There's no way around getting your heart broken, having money troubles every now and then, your kindness taken for weakness, your patience pushed to the tipping point. Or, having unforeseen events knock the wind right out of your sails. Life happens to the best of us. And if you are human you are bound to go through a human experience from time to time. There's not a whole lot you can do when all hell decides to break loose on you. But if you can remember not to panic but to keep your presence of mind, you'll develop the mental, emotional and spiritual fortitude you need to get your bearings, take inventory of your resources, figure out how to best survive the situation and plan a new course of action.

No matter what kind of pain we experience in life, we are equipped to handle it. It may not seem that way, but the truth is you have no other choice. As long as you are alive, life will happen while you're in the middle of living. However it works out for you, good, bad or ugly, know that you'll be ok. You are stronger than you know. Today, remind yourself that you are a survivor.

Wise Saying #14.
Sometimes You've Got To Take A Few Steps Back
In Order To Move Forward

The business you put your heart and soul in did not work out the way you planned. The job you gave twenty years of blood, sweat and tears to laid you off without a second thought. You thought you'd have a house, a husband, 2.5 kids and a few appreciating assets by now. Instead you've got two children out of wedlock. The three of you are living in a one-room rental and you don't have a dime to your name.

Sometimes our lives play out much differently than we imagine. And when this happens there's a tendency to beat ourselves up for not being where we thought we ought to be. Try not to should on yourself. Always remember that no matter where you are, you can make progress. There are golden opportunities all around you to see things a new way, try a new thing and make a fresh start. Instead of allowing yourself to sink into depression, ask yourself: *How can I grow from this experience and use it for my betterment? Knowing what I now know, what do I need to do moving forward?*

Sometimes it's helpful to think back to instances where you experienced a change or setback that you initially resisted but in the end worked out for your ultimate good. Perhaps it was being fired from a job. A transfer. A love relationship not working out the way you hoped. A new boss who was difficult and demanding—or any change that came your way that felt like it was the worst thing that could happen to you. Can you look back now and say, "I'm thankful it happened." Or, "I may not like that it had to happen to me, but I will use this experience to make the world a better place."

Today, know that sometimes taking a step back may actually be a push to move forward.

3

Holding On To Motherhood With Both Hands

Wise Saying #15.
Know That Love Is As Love Does

The most accurate measure of your success as a mother has nothing to do with how big your house is, how many assets you have, whether or not your children have the latest fashions or top brand name sneakers. It's not about whether or not your children attend private school, make the baseball team or ace the try-outs for the cheerleading squad. It's not about taking them to the best restaurants or spoiling them so rotten that they never learn how to be compassionate or humble.

Whether you live in a gated community, a trailer park, a one-room rental or a housing project with your sister and her kids, the true measure of your success as a mom is in knowing that love is as love does. What are you doing to demonstrate your love?

Do you love your children enough to come up higher or, if need be, get your act together? Do you love them enough to spend time with them, show them affection and encourage them to follow their dreams? Do you love them enough to check their homework, meet their friends and go up to the school to make your presence known? Do you love them enough to teach them to have manners, to say please and thank you and to treat others with kindness? Do you love them enough to pursue some of your own dreams so that you can be an example of excellence? Do you love them enough to discipline them and make sure they know right from wrong? Do you love them enough not to treat them like they're inconvenient, in the way or bothering you by wanting your time? How do you show your children that they are loved?

Wise Saying #16.
Take Your Role As Your Child's First Teacher Seriously

Children are like mini tape recorders. They take in everything they see and hear. At a very early age we are taught that small children should be seen and not heard. The problem with this way of parenting is if your children are never heard, then you will not know what's going on around them or inside of them. Obedience has its place and boundaries are important. But mindful, age-appropriate conversation is a necessary parenting skill.

What are your children taking in? Because everything they take in eventually comes out. If you stick them in front of a television set all day while you talk on the phone or get your groove on, it's only a matter of time before they start to repeat what they hear and act out what they see. Be careful of the conversations you have, even when you believe your children are not within earshot. You never know.

Always remember to find an outlet to deal with the pressures of being a single mom, otherwise you run the risk of coming home frustrated and on the edge. Be diligent about instilling self-respect, the importance of education and making morally responsible choices. At the end of the day, these are the things your children hold on to. Today, take your role as your child's first teacher seriously and ask yourself: *What am I teaching my child?*

Wise Saying #17.
Try Not To Blame Yourself For Your Children's Choices

When Brenda's son got himself arrested for selling drugs, she blamed herself and thought she was a bad mother. On the bus ride to jail, Brenda mentally rehashed all of the events leading up to her son's arrest and wondered where she went wrong. When Cynthia's fourteen-year-old daughter got pregnant, she blamed herself for putting in too many hours at the office. How could this happen? Cynthia and her daughter talked about everything and agreed that she would wait until she was married or at least out of high school before having sex. When Sarah's daughter started stealing from her to support her drug habit, she thought that these kinds of problems only happened in the ghetto, to urban, welfare moms. But circumstances never lie. Sarah was a college professor with two homes, one in the suburbs and the other in the Caribbean. She was getting married in the fall to a prominent pediatrician. So for all intents and purposes, this shouldn't be happening to her, but her situation is what it is.

Nothing makes a mother question her capabilities more deeply then when her children get into steep trouble and make choices that cause public humiliation. The truth is you can groom your children for greatness, teach them the basics, give them a firm foundation and they can still make bad choices. You can raise them in church, send them to the best schools, make sure that they want for nothing and sometimes in spite of all your hard work and good intentions, they still mess up … big time.

Try not to be too hard on yourself. You did the best that you could. All you can do from this point on is love your children and be there for them. Always remember, no matter how far your children decide to stray, they still need to know you love them.

Wise Saying #18.
Let Your Praise Outweigh Your Criticism

As a parent who wants the best for your child, it's easy to get so caught up in pushing your son or daughter to excel that you criticize more than you praise. More than anything else, your children need your love and acceptance. A critical remark, a harsh statement or an insensitive comment made in jest can take root in your children and cause them to believe that they are not capable, lovable or worthy. Or, that nothing they do is good enough. Constant criticism breeds self-doubt and fans the flames of insecurity. While it's important that you motivate your children to be the very best, be mindful not to be so hard to please that you become the perpetual judge and jury.

Every parent wants the best for their kids. But keep in mind that it takes an average of four praiseworthy comments to undo the harm of one negative one. Try to catch your children doing something right. Point out their strengths. Notice the good that they do. When you let your praise outweigh your criticism, you sow the seeds of healthy self-esteem.

Wise Saying #19.
Acknowledge Your Children's Need To Talk About
And Spend Time With Their Dad

It's easy to downplay the significance of the other parent, especially if he's only minimally involved or doesn't bother with his kids at all. It's important for you to know that just because your child's father might be physically absent from your home does not mean that he is absent from your child's heart and mind.

If your child's father wants to be involved, don't stand in the way. The only one who loses out are the children. Even if you believe that he is selfish and irresponsible, if this is true, the children will find this out for themselves in due time. But if you stand in the way, they'll resent you for many years to come.

Study after study shows that children who have relationships with both of their parents fair better than those who do not. The bottom line here is no matter how you feel about your child's father, acknowledge the children's need to talk about and spend time with him.

Wise Saying #20.
Don't Allow Guilt To Cause You To Overcompensate

You look at your children and you don't want them to suffer or want for anything. You work hard to put food on the table, keep a roof over their heads and let them know how much they are loved. Perhaps you work long hours and don't get to spend as much time with your children as you would like. You might even feel like the children have one strike against them because they do not have both of their parents living under the same roof. Be careful about allowing guilt to get the best of you. Because guilt can cause you to worry about things you cannot control, live beyond your means or overcompensate by giving into your children's every whim.

What your children need most are your love, time and attention. Have fun with them. Play dress up. Take them to the beach, park or museum. Spend an afternoon in the library. Exercise as a family. Go to an outdoor concert. Have a family picnic on your living room floor. Turn on the music and dance. Cook together. Go on a nature walk. Create a new tradition like: bike riding on Saturday, pizza night on Friday. The goal here is to create special moments and memories together.

For many single mothers, there's a tendency to feel pressured around birthdays and holidays. Take the pressure off by creating simple family traditions and learning the true meaning of the holiday. Cherished customs give children something to look forward to and something meaningful to hold on to. So don't worry about keeping up with the Jones's. As long as your children are well fed, warmly dressed, safely sheltered and loved, they'll be just fine. In fact, a little doing without teaches children about money management, delaying gratification, the value of people over possessions and the strength of character that comes with not having everything handed to you on a silver platter.

Wise Saying #21.
Give Them Wings To Fly

Love them unconditionally and they will learn to love themselves.
Praise them often and they will believe that they can move mountains.
Catch them doing something right and they will do more good.
Instill honesty and they will tell the truth.
Teach them to respect themselves and they will respect others.
Teach them to think for themselves and they will stand their ground when pressured to sway away.
Let them help around the house and they will be self-sufficient.
Encourage them to imagine and they will see the possibilities
Keep the lines of communication open and they will rarely shut you out.
Teach them the value of a dollar and they will be able to make it on their own.
Stress the importance of staying grounded and they will walk the way of humility.
Teach them to have integrity and they will do the right thing.
Teach them to be kind and they will be keepers of peace.
Teach them to dream big dreams and they will leave a legacy for generations to come.

Cassandra Mack

4

Coming Up Higher

Wise Saying #22.
Be A Class Act

Class acts come in all shapes and sizes. They come from every walk of life. From every wrung on the socio-economic ladder. I'll bet that there have been times when you've seen a woman walk into the room with such style and grace that everyone stopped and took notice. Sometimes you can't put your finger on all of the qualities that makes a class act stand out, but you definitely know a class act when you see one. When I think of women like: Felicia Rashad, from the Cosby Show, the late Jackie O, Tyra Banks, CeCe Winans and Susan Taylor from Essence magazine, I think of class acts.

Class acts distinguish themselves by their values, their way of thinking and their standards of behavior. A class act displays grace under pressure and carries herself with the utmost respect. She genuinely likes herself so it's easy for her to radiate confidence and poise. A class act is not boastful, but she does not dim her light either. She has integrity and manages to hold on to her dignity even in the middle of strife and confusion.

How can you come across as a class act? Simple. By doing these five things consistently:

1. Commit to excellence.
2. Choose to live by a higher set of standards.
3. Counteract pettiness with tact.
4. Command a higher level of respect by treating everyone you know with compassion and dignity.
5. Raise the quality of your thinking.

Wise Saying #23.
Let Go Of Habits That Do Not Serve You Well

If you practice a behavior consistently enough it becomes a habit. The problem with habits are we do them without thinking about it. And whenever we are not thinking about what we are doing, we may not see the harmful effects of our behavior. This is why it is so important that you pay attention to your habits, especially the ones that do not serve you well. So the question I pose to you is: Are your habits serving you well? If not, it might be well worth the effort to make a few changes. Start by taking an inventory of your habits. Identify the ones that are self-destructive or undesirable and develop the willpower to eliminate them from your life.

Bad habits can be your worst enemy, if they get in the way of your health, happiness and success. Almost everything you do is a result of your habits, from your morning routine, to what you eat, to the way you wear your hair, to what you do with your time.

The most powerful way to get rid of a bad habit is to adopt new behaviors that are more in line with what you want to have, how you want to feel and where you want to be in life. If you really set your mind to it and adopt the attitude that nothing will stand in your way, you can cast aside the habits that are not consistent with the type of person you want to become.

Wise Saying #24.
Get Your Self-Esteem Into High Gear

Every now and then we all need to spring clean our self-esteem in order to get it into high gear. It's important to periodically check in with yourself to make sure that you have the mental and emotional fortitude to do the things you need to do to live a full and joyful life. It's also important that you do things that lift your spirits up and that make you feel good about yourself.

Your achievements, effectiveness as a person and your ability to overcome difficult obstacles are governed, for the most part, by how you feel about yourself and how forcefully you act on your beliefs. Here are some tips to help you get your self-esteem into high gear.

1. Keep Learning

Learn something new each day. The average American reads a book a year, so if you read two you're technically above average. Watch the discovery and biography channels. Take a class. Attend a workshop. Surf the net.

2. Surround Yourself With Positive People

Cultivate relationships with people who motivate you, cheer you on, support you and challenge you to rise higher.

3. Turn Your Inner Critic Into Your Inner Coach

Counteract negative thoughts with more positive, reaffirming ones. Look around for motivational mottos and make them your mantras. Be aware of your internal chatter and keep it in check.

4. Keep Things In Perspective

Be realistic about what you can and cannot do given your responsibilities, resources at hand and time constraints. Then, do what you can do.

Wise Saying #25.
Get Out Of Your Comfort Zone

If you want to achieve radical results you've got to do something that you've never done before—something that stretches you, forces you to grow, builds your skills, pulls out your potential and challenges you to rise to higher heights. And whatever you do, you cannot allow fear to hold you back.

Far too often, fear is the only thing that stands in the way of you and your dreams. We come into this world with only two fears: the fear of falling and the fear of loud noises. All other fears are learned responses.

Fear is one of the most dangerous time bandits. Why? Because fear discourages you from pursuing your dreams, trying new things and it causes you to stay in situations that you have outgrown. Whenever you feel fearful of trying something new or difficult, remind yourself that you have what it takes to make it. If that doesn't work feel the fear and do it anyway. What have you got to lose? Today, take the plunge and get out of your comfort zone.

Wise Saying #26.
Be A Good Steward Over Your Gift of Time

When was the last time you stopped to think about how your time was being spent and how you felt about it? Between work, commuting back and forth to work, spending quality time with the kids, cooking, cleaning, running errands, going over homework, grocery shopping, taking care of yourself and so on, your time is probably in very short supply. As a single mom, your choices around how you spend your time become even more important because you have less of it to go around.

One of the ways to take greater control over how you spend your time is to set priorities in the form of a top five list. Different from goal setting, your top five list is a list of priorities that need your time and attention now and that if you take care of right way, you'll free up more time to do the things you want to do. Try to get in the habit of taking five minutes each day to create a weekly and daily top five list. Be sure to place working on your dreams and caring for yourself on this list.

In addition to helping you focus on what's important, your top five list will enable you to say no to the things that you need to start saying no to so that you can start saying yes to you. Most importantly, it enables you to protect one of your most precious resources—your gift of time.

Wise Saying #27.
Find Out What Makes You Happy

No matter what your definition of happiness is, it is your responsibility to find out what makes you happy. Each of us has our own definition of happiness. Some say it's in finding what interests you and doing it well. Others believe it's something you look forward to. For me, it's about enjoying everyday life and feeling contented on the inside no matter what's going on around me. How do you define happiness? If you were to respond to the sentence stem, "I would be happy if_____." What would you say?

Knowing exactly what you need to feel fulfilled and contented is the starting point for living a happy life. Through introspection and self-reflection, you should be able to figure out what makes you happy. Sometimes we fail to notice how happy we are because we are so busy looking for external signs and the next big thrill that we don't pay attention to the good in our lives. If you make it a point to count your blessings and enjoy the little things, you will probably come to find that you discovered the secret to true happiness a long time ago.

Wise Saying #28.
Develop A Millionaire's Mindset

We can't talk about success in life without talking about financial success, because whatever your goals, be they: going back to school, purchasing a home, taking a trip, buying a new dining room set, turning your hobby into a money-making business, paying for your child to take piano lessons or saving for your kids college tuition, they all cost money. The good news is financial success starts in the mind. It's about deciding what you want. This includes sitting down with pen and paper in hand and seriously thinking about how much you want to earn, save and invest. Second, you have to believe that it is possible to accumulate wealth and live prosperously. Third, you must learn all that you can about money and how it operates. Lastly, you have to make sacrifices and get your children involved with the plan.

One of the first rules to becoming wealthy is to make a conscious decision to do so. As women, we work too hard, get paid too little and never seem to get ahead. The remedy to this problem is changing our mindset and moving from striving for survival to striving for wealth. There's nothing wrong with setting your mind on becoming wealthy as long as you don't sell your soul in the process.

Wealth means different things to different people, but the quickest way to get clear about your financial goals is to put an exact dollar figure on how much you want to earn, save and invest each year, each month and each week. So, how much do you want to earn, save and invest? How much do you want to have when you retire? How much money will you need to maintain your current lifestyle when you stop working? How much debt do you owe and what steps do you need to take to get yourself out of debt? What kind of financial head start do you want to provide for your child?

Get serious about your money. Become financially literate. You cannot afford to be in the dark about your finances. Don't live beneath your privilege by living beyond your means. Build assets instead of liabilities. Make more before you spend more. Turn your financial situation around by tithing. And remember there are many ways to tithe. Contribute a portion of your income to your place of worship or a social cause that you believe in. If you cannot tithe money, you can tithe your time. Volunteer for a good cause. Donate clothing and toys that are in good-as-new condition to your local charity or a family who is in need of the items you have.

The lesson here is no matter how financially strapped you are, you always have something to give. And this is how the millionaire's mindset begins.

5

Letting Go of Excess Baggage

Wise Saying #29.
Don't Let Bitterness Get The Best of You

When I was in the thick of what I call my hateful season, all I did was talk about how wrong and mean-spirited my son's father was, mentally rehash all of the details of every, little argument we ever had and fantasize about the many ways that I could pay him back for all the hell he gave to me. I went to bed angry and woke up with an attitude. The more I focused my time and energy on the animosity between us, the more I become poisoned by my own hate. I suffered from migraines, nosebleeds, backaches and muscle spasms.

And while everything I complained about was true, my constant agonizing over his bad behavior was taking its' toll on me. See the thing of it is whenever we get stuck in anger, our focus shifts from living our best lives and being fully engaged with our children to perfecting the art of war and devising payback strategies so we can get even. This keeps us bitter and leaves no room for the good to come in.

There's a price we pay when we allow bitterness to seep in and engage in tit-for-tat tactics. Even if the anger is justified or we believe the other person had it coming. What begins to happen is that same bitterness spirals into the other facets of our lives causing a domino effect. And sooner than you know it, it starts to dominate your thoughts, consume your conversations and pollute your entire spirit. It also depletes you of your drive to move beyond the mindset of powerlessness. It simply cost too much to be bitter. So if bitterness is taking its toll on you, ask yourself: How much is this really costing me?

Wise Saying #30.
Forgiveness Doesn't Mean Defeat

One of life's greatest teaching tools was to give us the power to remember the past, without the power to go back and change it. This provides us with an authentic opportunity for spiritual growth. The power to remember the past without the ability to change it seems like a double-edged sword especially when it comes to practicing the principle of forgiveness.

Forgiving someone who has hurt or betrayed you is not easy. It's even harder to forgive someone you love. But, when you choose to forgive instead of holding on to old resentments, you give yourself a priceless gift—the gift of freedom. When you forgive you literally set yourself free. As long as you refuse to forgive you are still emotionally tied to the pain of the experience as well as the person who wronged you.

So what does forgiveness mean? It means three things:

1. Giving up the desire to get even
After someone has hurt you, betrayed you or pissed you off in any way, the natural inclination is to try and get even. We want the other person to feel our pain, get a taste of their own medicine and pay the piper big time. But the problem with being tit-for-tat is you can never truly get even. You can cause pain, devastation and destruction but you cannot get even. What's done is done. It's fine to want justice. It's perfectly reasonable to fight for it. But there's a fine line between justice and revenge.

2. Disconnecting from the painful feelings tied to the experience
It's perfectly healthy to be angry with someone who has wronged you, but it's very unhealthy to let negative feelings fester and contaminate your soul. There comes a time when you have to come to terms with the experience and make a commitment to release the

negative feelings. As long as you have negative feelings festering in your heart, you are still spiritually and emotionally tied to the person. You cannot move forward until you make peace with your past. Even if you are 110% right and the other person is 200 X dead wrong, holding on to negativity will only poison you.

3. Understanding that the person who hurt you is a child of God even if he or she doesn't act like it
We are all children of God. Some of us act like it more than others, but we are all God's creations. When we demonize another human being we make them larger than life and give them more power in our lives than they deserve. When we recognize them for who and what they are—a child of God in pain, we can begin to de-personalize their actions and decrease their significance in our lives. This allows us to reclaim our power and to understand that hurting people often hurt people. This does not mean that we ought to diminish the seriousness of their actions or allow ourselves to be walking doormats. It means that we should try real hard to refuse to allow the individual or their actions to have any more power over us.

Wise Saying #31.
Choose Your Battles

The child support check is late, again. The children need winter coats and your ex is crying broke, again. He cancelled a visit with the children, again. He left the explicit CD in the car, again. He brought that trifling hussy around your kids, again. And you are sick and tired of the drama and trauma. Usually when these kinds of things happen, there's a tendency to lose your cool and prepare for battle. But most of the time, it's just not worth it. I'm not saying that you shouldn't speak your piece, hold people accountable for their actions or refuse to be taken for a ride. I'm merely saying that you should pick your battles.

Sometimes you may feel perfectly justified in letting someone "really have it." But after you've had a moment to calm down and carefully look back at the situation, you may regret your actions. You may think that by arguing your point or going out of your way to prove how right you are, that you come out on top. But more often than not, the other person will either tune you out or do something even more stupid to piss you off even more.

Anger is a powerful emotion and when you go into conflict mode over every little issue, you allow that anger to build up like a pot of boiling water waiting to explode. In the end the other person has gotten the best of you. Sometimes you have to just let things go. This does not mean that you should let people walk all over you. It simply means that you'd be better off if you didn't let other people get to you as often. There are better ways to deal with people who say and do things that upset you. When you are calm, you can tell the other person how you feel and explain how the children are impacted by their actions. You can exercise your legal rights. You can have your attorney contact his attorney. Just don't make a public fool of yourself.

Before battling it out with someone stop and ask yourself, "What will I gain by blowing my lid?"

Wise Saying #32.
Don't Become The Neighborhood Soap Opera

Vicki knew that there was no turning back when she threw her son's father's clothes out the window of their fifth floor apartment and spray painted the word *DOG* on the windshield of his car. But she didn't care. According to Vicki he had it coming. He was a liar and a cheat and she had had enough. The neighbors were talking. The children were watching. And Vicki was just getting started.

The courtroom scene was even worse. He called her a conniving bitch and a whore. She called him every four letter word in the book. The lawyers told them both to settle down. But Vicki had reached her tipping point. She made fun of his lack of education. Talked about his mean-spirited mother. And shouted at the top of her lungs that he was loser who couldn't get it up in bed. That's when the court officers came over and threatened to take her out of the building in handcuffs if she did not calm herself down.

Normally, Vicki is a very, classy lady. She's cultured, educated and thoroughly refined. But everybody has their breaking point. However, the problem with breaking in public is it causes you to spiral out of control and it makes you look like a prime candidate for Child Protective Services. So unless you are auditioning for the Jerry Springer show, you'd do best to save the drama for the movies.

Wise Saying #33.
Give Yourself Time To Grieve

When we lose someone we love to physical death, we understand that it is perfectly normal to grieve. But when we suffer the death of a relationship, we tell ourselves that we should just get over it, move on with our lives and get right back out there and date again. A loss is a loss. And if you lose someone you love, you will grieve for them. You will go through the typical stages. First comes shock: *This isn't really happening.* Then comes denial: *This can't be happening to me.* Next comes anger: *That bastard will pay. If it's the last thing I do.* Then comes confusion: *I don't know what to do.* Then comes fear: *How will I make it on my own? Will I ever love again? Will anyone still find me attractive?* Then comes numbness: *Nothing matters anymore. I don't have the strength to fight or care.* And finally comes acceptance: *I'm ok with it. Whatever happens I'll be all right.*

Take the time you need to grieve. When you give yourself time to grieve, you allow yourself to release the negative thoughts and emotions that eventually enable you to accept the situation for what it is. And this enables you to move on. Today, take the time you need to grieve.

Wise Saying #34.
You Can Love Someone and Still To Let Them Go

You can love someone and still need to let them go. You can be madly and passionately head over heels with someone who can't or won't give you what you want and need. You can make sacrifices, give the best years of your life and make beautiful children and still never get past go. You can have mind-blowing, bone-chilling, over-the-mountaintop-sex and when it's all said and done it was nothing more than a ready-made booty call that he got on the regular. They say the definition of insanity is continuing to do the same thing but expecting different results. What do you call staying in a relationship that tears away at your self-esteem, leaves you wondering if you are worthy and capable or makes you happy sometimes and sad most of the time?

It's not healthy or productive to stay in a relationship that does not meet your emotional and spiritual needs. It's self-defeating to lie to yourself when the truth of your situation is starring you smack in the face. It's downright foolish to hang in there when it's evident by his actions that he doesn't love you, you're not a top priority for him or he's simply just not that into you. You can tell yourself he loves you, but he's too afraid to show it. Or, that he wants to find the right time to break the news to his wife. But, always remember that love is as love does and you deserve a healthy relationship with someone who thinks the world of you.

Wise Saying #35.
Don't Bring Old Baggage Into A New Relationship

There are no guarantees in life, but you can safely bet that if you bring old baggage into a new relationship your relationship is destined for trouble. If you constantly accuse him of cheating when he hasn't done anything, call him a liar when he tells the truth and cling to him for dear life when he needs a little space, eventually he's going to get tired. Tired of trying to prove himself. Tired of being grilled and tired of having to pacify your never-ending neediness and insecurity. When you focus your time and energy on what you do not want you usually get the very thing that you're trying to avoid. When you concentrate on trying to catch him out there, wait for him to mess up or question him over and over about the same issue to see if the story changes, you start to look paranoid and controlling. And who wants to be around someone who is paranoid and controlling?

If trust is an issue for you, work on it. If being vulnerable is an issue, work on it. If being taken advantage of is an issue for you, don't allow yourself to be used. If your mother was controlling and your father was never there for you, you're a grown woman now, so it is your responsibility to work on your issues. Nobody's perfect. Everyone has an issue or two to contend with. But if your issues are coming between your health, happiness and peace of mind, then it's time to put in the work to make yourself healthier, happier and whole. Whether you join a support group, find a good therapist, journal and meditate or undergo strict spiritual study, do what you need to do to lay your baggage to rest.

6

Sex and The Single Mom

Wise Saying #36.
Keep Yourself Up

It's 10:00 o'clock on a Saturday morning. You're at the supermarket shopping for a few items You figure not too many people will be out and about since it's still early, so there's no harm done if you throw on your old baggy sweats with the chocolate stained t-shirt. You even wrap a wrinkled scarf around your head for good measure. As you're walking down the third aisle taste testing the grapes, in walks the man of your dreams. He's tall. He's handsome. He's of age. He's got all his teeth. No wedding ring. And no visible signs of psychosis. He looks up at you and smiles. You want to smile back and get your flirt on. But, you look down at your granny sweat pants and feel too embarrassed to reply.

We all know that in the end it is what's on the inside that truly counts. And for the most part, this is true. But by now you also know good and well that no self-respecting man wants a sloppy, raggedy looking woman who doesn't care enough about herself to at least make the effort to look neat and presentable. I'm not saying that you have to look like you're ready to hit the runway each and every time you walk out your door. Or, that you'll get a summons from the fashion police for an occasional backslide. But at the same time you shouldn't look like you just crawled out of bed without showering, combing your hair or ironing your clothes either.

When a man first meets you he cannot see your heart, your winning personality and all the good things you have to offer. The only thing he has to go on is his first impression of you, in essence, the way you look. First impressions really do matter. So hook it up, girl. Be the queen that you are. Don't dare be seen in public looking like you've just stuck your finger in an electrical outlet or come down with a bad case of the flu. It's not about putting on a show for someone else. It's about thinking enough of yourself to treat yourself special every day.

As a single mom, it's easy to get caught up in the routine of the daily grind and believe that since it's just you and the kids, there's no good reason to take the time dress neatly, wear your hair in a flattering style or pamper yourself from the inside out, but the truth is when you look better you feel better. And it shows. You radiate confidence and become more attractive and magnetic no matter what age or size. So go on down to the mall and buy yourself some scented lotion, a new blouse or that funky little dress that shows off your curves. Throw on your sexy jeans with the form-fitting jacket. Clip on your 18-inch ponytail. Glue your false eyelashes on. Then, work it and watch them sweat.

Wise Saying #37.
Your Kids Come First

Your kids come first. Don't ever let your quest to find or keep a man drive you to put your children on the backburner, ship them off to your mother's so they're out of the way or force them to like him in order to create an instant, ready-made family. Because if he truly is the one, things will progress naturally, in due time. He will also come to love your children as if they were his own.

As a single mom you need to remember that when you get seriously involved with a man, your potential Mr. Right has to understand that this is a package deal. There's no way around it because the children live with you. And if the relationship is moving towards marriage, then all of you will be living under the same roof. So if things start to get serious, at some point, you'll need to discuss how a blended-family will work for the two of you.

Most of all, remember that your sex life is your private business, so your children should not be exposed to a revolving door of boyfriends. You can date, hang out and get your swerve on, but do it away from home until the relationship moves toward commitment. And here's a news flash: Three months of steady sex is not a commitment.

Unless he is proposing or making preparations to build a home with you and your children, you do not have a commitment. So take things slow. Find out about his character. His goals and life plans. Make sure he's good to your children and that you trust him around your children. In this day and age, it's not a bad idea to check into a man's background. You can do a web-based search, get to know his friends and family and if you know of a previous wife or girlfriend, tactfully ask her about him. It's not about being paranoid. It's about ensuring that your children are safe and making sure that the man you plan to let into your home and heart is who he claims to be.

Wise Saying #38.
It's OK To Keep Your Legs Closed

So far you've been on three dates with him. He's cute, funny and gainfully employed. You genuinely like him. He looks deep into your eyes. Tells you that you're beautiful. Caresses your cheek all the way home. Opens the car door for you. Walks you to your apartment door. Gently kisses you on the forehead. Then asks if it would be all right to come upstairs for a nightcap. The children are with their father this weekend. You're feeling kind of woozy. It has been a long, long, long time since you've had some. What do you do? There's only one answer: You wait!!!

I know. I know. It's a new day and you're a modern woman. So what could possibly be wrong with letting him break you off a little something, something? Plenty. For starters, if you want him to keep you in the running for a serious relationship, you cannot sell yourself short. While certainly there are a few exceptions and you can probably think of one or two girlfriends who gave up the goods on the first date and are now happily married. Remember, this is the exception. Not the rule. And while your stuff may be pretty exceptional, at the end of the day it's just sex. You haven't given him anything of real substance to hold on to and to make him feel like you could be an asset worth serious consideration.

I'm not saying that he will object to having sex with you it if you let him, even the good ones rarely refuse easy sex. He may even ask to see you again if it was good. But don't confuse sexual chemistry with intimacy. Although most men will not say this to your face, especially if they are trying to have sex with you, if you make it too easy, then they have no incentive to stay around for the long haul. It's not about playing games or having a rigid set of rules that don't feel right for you. It's about giving yourself enough time to make sure that he's really worth it and that you wont have any regrets—that you wont feel like you made a mistake, got in over your head or played yourself. Time really does reveal most things.

And don't allow the fear of him getting it from somewhere else make you have sex before you are ready. He's a grown man. Chances are he was already getting it from somewhere else when he met you. That's not your issue just yet. Let the other women play the position of booty call. You position yourself for wife.

The best sex, involves taking intimacy to the next level. But the next level implies that there was a mental, emotional and spiritual foundation to begin with. Sex is a beautiful thing. Be that as it may. It's still perfectly ok to keep your legs closed.

Wise Saying #39.
If He Did It To Her, He'll Do It To You

He put her through the wringer. Dragged her through the mud. Disrespected her to the tenth degree. Denied that the kids were his. Refuses to be bothered with his children. Talks about her like a dog. Even calls her out of her name. Says she's a no good whore who got pregnant on purpose. As if she was able to carry out this feat by herself. Whenever she calls about the children, he's rude and downright nasty. Plays her messages for you to hear. You laugh. Call her stupid. On occasion, you chime in to set the record straight. Agree that she's a gold digger out to take all of his money. When the truth of the matter is she is only asking for what legally belongs to her child.

The irony of it all is, you say that she's the stupid one, but you're the one who is standing by his side, supporting his ignorant and irresponsible behavior. Many women feel that they don't owe it to another woman, especially their man's ex, to show a little respect and refuse to engage in catty, uncalled for behavior. You don't owe it to her. You owe it to yourself. Because when you respect and think highly of yourself, you wont even think about stepping to her to start some nonsense. And if you honestly believe she's a low down drama queen, and you think you're above her behavior, then wouldn't it make sense to refuse to engage in catfights or spend your time and energy talking about her?

The hardest thing for the average woman who doesn't want to be alone to understand is if he did it to her, he'll do it to you. If it is in his character to be deceitful, disrespectful, mean, controlling, selfish or violent, then the traits are still there. He just hasn't exercised them with you yet. Perhaps he told you that you were different. He's normally not this angry, it's just that she got under his skin and brought out the worst in him. But you're better than her. Classier. More understanding. Less demanding. You make crispier chicken. Your breath smells fresher. You're freakier in bed. Take him through less changes. Got a nicer body. And you bought every word of it: hook, line and sinker.

The best predictor of future behavior is past behavior. I'm not saying that people cannot change. They can. But I'm sure you know by now that if it talks like a leopard, walks like a leopard and acts like a leopard, chances are, it still has leopard tendencies. So as you laugh at his jokes, listen to him disrespect her, ride around in the car that took food from his children's mouths, or hold the hands that used to beat her down, just remember, you could be next.

Wise Saying #40.
You're Strong, Independent, All That and A Bag of Chips But Is Your Attitude Keeping You Alone?

You're intelligent. Attractive. And fully capable of holding your own. You've got an MBA, your own home in the suburbs or you're renting a great apartment with a fabulous view. You've got a 401K plan, a nice size savings. You've even taken yourself on vacation for the past couple of years. And you did it all on your own. Many would say you've got it going on big time. You say, you are just doing you. There's only one problem: For the past five years you've been sitting home alone and you'd really like to meet someone nice who has the potential to be your Mr. Right.

But you've got your requirements. You wont even think about dating a man unless he has a college degree, works a white collard job making close to six figures, drives a nice car, moves comfortably in the most influential social circles, dresses well, has a perfect command of the English language, is not too nerdy but not to thugged-out either, is taller than you by at least four inches, doesn't talk too loud, watch too much TV or have any other bad habits that get on your nerves. And preferably, no kids. That's a tall order. And the older we get, the harder that order becomes to fill. Don't get me wrong. There's nothing wrong with having standards. Just make sure that your standards are not so rigorous and inflexible that they're keeping you alone.

There's nothing wrong with wanting a man who's got it going on externally. But you also want to make sure that he has the character and decency to back it up. Is he kind, thoughtful, honest, caring, hardworking and family oriented? How does he treat your children? Does he value and respect you? Maybe he drives a Honda instead of a BMW or he works with his hands instead of giving orders from an office. Maybe he doesn't have a college degree but he's intelligent, articulate and socially conscious. Just maybe he doesn't have all of the external features that you're looking for but he's a great guy who works hard, brings home a check, has integrity, is a good conversationalist and thinks the world of you and your children. Would you be willing to pass him up in favor of a guy who had it going on externally but treated you like crap, was dismissive towards your children and acted like he was doing you a favor by showing you a little interest.

See it's not about lowering your standards. It's about re-examining your priorities so that you look deeper than a man's education and pockets. Sometimes you've got to sit down with yourself to figure out what's really important to you in a mate, especially when you think long term. Life is too short to allow rigorous standards to keep you alone.

Wise Saying #41.
Does He Love You Enough To Wipe Your Behind?

My grandmother, Elsie Lee Daglow, was one of the wisest women I knew. She grew up in a small town in South Hill, Virginia in the 1920's and came to New York in search of a better life. My grandmother came from good stock—generations of strong Black women who did what they had to do to survive and create a better life for their children. My grandmother was married twice and had ten children. Seven that she gave birth to and three that she inherited from her second husband. She didn't have much money, but she was rich beyond measure.

Before she died, we would have long talks around the kitchen table. She'd be frying chicken or making sweet potato biscuits, while I helped and tried to soak up her love and wisdom. As we broached the subject of love, she said: *Before you give your heart to a man, make sure he loves you enough to wipe your behind?* After being thoroughly mortified by the images that came to mind, I tried to slowly take in what my grandmother meant by this and asked her if she could explain this wise old saying to me. She said: *When you are young and naïve, you're concerned with flowers, candy and getting butterflies in your stomach when he walks into the room. But as you have children and get older those things become less important and it's really about the character of a man, the way he cares for you and stands by you when the chips are down. Everyday ain't going to be a party. But at the end of the day, do you trust him to stick with you when things get rough and ugly, to care for you in the dirtiest places? That's real love, the kind that you can count on when you're sick, frail, not as pretty as you used to be, if you ever get into an accident that robs you of your independence and mobility, when you're broke, broken and when life beats you down. See baby, love is not a feeling. It is choosing to be good to the one you claim to love.*

So in the words of my wise old grandmother: When you meet a man who you believe could be the one, ask yourself, *Does he love me enough to wipe my behind?*

Wise Saying #42.
The Best Kind of Loving Starts With Self Love

What does healthy love feel like? I have asked myself this very same question a million times and the more I get to know and love myself the clearer the answer becomes. I believe that healthy love starts from a position of self-love. It's about being consistent with yourself, knowing what you want and need out of life, accepting yourself totally—the good, the bad and the ugly. It's in knowing that there will be days when you do not feel like being supportive, respectful or kind to yourself but if you are choosing to live in love then you do what you gotta do, period, end of story. Real love is not something that you fall and blindly slip into. It is something that you thoughtfully, work at and cultivate. Romance fades. Passion wanes. Attraction come and goes. But real love lives on.

Love is not flowers, candy or even passionate sex. These things are actions that one takes to show appreciation and keep the romance alive, but flowers, candy or any other external gifts are not true testaments of love. Love is showing appreciation, being kind, respectful and valuing one another, supporting each other's goals, dreams and development while giving each other room to grow. Love is being trustworthy as well as trusting your partner. Love is a consistent and constant demonstration of your commitment to one another. So I ask you, before you go out looking for a partner to love, have you loved yourself lately?

Conclusion

Being a single mom isn't easy. Your time is limited. Your resources are stretched. And money is often tight. You'll have obstacles to overcome and hurdles to climb, but you can do it. You can be a good mother, a whole person, live a full life and leave a legacy for your children, because you already have everything you need to succeed. You've got children who love you, a God who's watching over you and sheer determination to keep you moving forward.

Remember the basics—faith, belief in self, discipline and balance. Remember that nobody's better than you and no one is more deserving than you. Always count your blessings, even in the midst of a crisis. Don't forget to smell the roses. Take time to play. And tell your children that you love them, often.

Hold on to your dignity and joy. When it's all said and done no one can take these things away from you. Life is waiting for you to answer your call. So go ahead and follow your heart. See you on the path....

About the Author

Cassandra Mack, MSW is a trained social worker, empowerment coach, business seminar leader, and founder of *Savvy Single Moms*, an on-line networking and resource sharing group geared for single mothers of color. She is the producer and host of *The No More Drama Hour of Power,* an online talk radio show of the New York Carib News. You can listen to her show by going to the *Savvy Single Moms* website: **www.savvysinglemoms.net** and clicking on the show link.

Cassandra has written five other books: *Cool, Confident and Strong: 52 Power Moves for Girls, Young Gifted and Doing It: 52 Power Moves for Teens, Smart Moves That Successful Youth Workers Make, Smart Moves That Successful Managers Make* and *Her Rite of Passage: How To Design A Rites of Passage Program for African-American Girls.* Cassandra has appeared on Good Day New York, What Women Want, Teen Talk and numerous radio programs.

She has written for the New York Beacon, Belle magazine, Guidelines, Proud Poppa and has presented keynotes and workshops at national conventions and conferences. Cassandra's expertise comes from a blend of experience as a single mother, social worker, parenting group facilitator, a former youth service practitioner and business owner. Cassandra lives in New York with her son, Briston and their goldfish Elmo. If you would like to contact Cassandra about conducting a keynote or break-out session for your special event or to find out more about *Savvy Single Moms* go to: **www.savvysinglemoms.net**

Savvy Single Moms Success Tour

An exciting, interactive, lunchtime, seminar-series, that will kick off in New York City, then travel to Baltimore and Washington DC. Bring a brown bag lunch and join us for 90-minutes of empowerment, success-strategizing and candid dialogue.

Please check the **Savvy Single Moms** website: **www.savvysinglemoms.net** for dates, times and locations.

Our purpose here is threefold: First, to provide you with a forum for connecting, sharing and information gathering. Second to provide you with a framework for healing and insight for empowerment. Third, to provide you with tools that you can utilize to develop a game-plan for lifelong success and achievement.

Some of our sessions will be open to men. This way you can get your personal growth on and your groove on at the same time. Hey! We're single mothers with enormous time constraints and childcare challenges. What better way to kill two birds with one stone: personal empowerment and meeting interesting, eligible men. You never know? You just might make a love connection.

Each ninety-minute seminar will begin with an interactive, ice-breaker so that you can mix, mingle and network. We'll also leave some time at the end for Q & A. Here's a sampling of what we'll be offering.

- **Escaping the Bitter Baby's Mama Trap:** How to Avoid Five Fatal Mistakes Smart Single Moms Make

- **I'm Smart, Competent and Sharp … So Why Am I Not Where I Want To Be Yet?**

- **Holding On to Motherhood With Both Hands:** How To Rightfully Balance Giving To Your Children Without Totally Depleting Yourself

Coming Soon ...

◆

The Single Moms Little Book Series

- **The Single Moms Little Book of Comfort and Joy:** Self-care Strategies and Pampering Principles To Help You Recharge, Renew and Revive

- **The Single Moms Little Book of Financial Empowerment:** How To Make Ends Meet, Build Wealth and Live Prosperously

- **The Single Moms Little Book of Dating, Relating, Mating and Cohabitating:** How To Spot The Good Ones, Avoid The Losers, Get The Odds To Work In Your Favor and Make A Blended Family Work for You

Please check our website for details: **www.savvysinglemoms.net**

978-0-595-39752-5
0-595-39752-2

LaVergne, TN USA
29 December 2010
210538LV00005B/17/A